Against All Odds

Against All Odds

The compelling story of

Macclesfield Town's

epic struggle from non

league obscurity to full

football league status

PHOTOGRAPHY: PAUL ATHERTON

TEXT: NEIL HOWARTH & DAVID LAFFERTY

Foreword

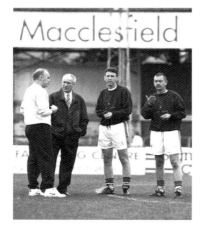

WELL, the odds were actually 12-1 but nobody could really believe that by the end of the season Macclesfield Town would have achieved so much in the Nationwide Third Division, and be promoted as runners - up. In these days of tens of thousands of pounds per week for the Premier League players, a visit to Macclesfield reveals the other side of football, where everybody knows everybody else and fans and players can mingle together after a game without the presence of agents and hangers on.

When I first thought of this project over three years ago as the team climbed up to the top of the Vauxhall Conference only to have their rightful place in the Football League denied, I knew that the first year in the League would be eventful no matter what happened.

Some people have also said that I should carry on and document the next season. It was always my intention to document the first season of a new club in the league . Next season, Macclesfield will be seen as a real threat and a team with form rather than a team that is new and, accordingly, the atmosphere will change. I hope for the sake of the fans that not too many things change (apart from the toilets!) but there is already talk of every game being all ticket due to the limited space.

I only hope that the step up to Div 2 isn't just about survival rather than an adventure because that's what this season has been. However, I feel that for the club to be successful, both on and off the pitch, this will mean a move toward the Corporate Client with the possible alienation of the die hard Macclesfield fan.

At one point during the past season I overheard Sammy McIlroy bemoaning the fact that a game had to be cancelled due to the covers not being put on soon enough to insulate the pitch and saying that the club "still had one foot in the Conference". Perhaps this is the secret - remember where you have come from but dream of where you might get to.

So with the season ahead we can look forward to some big name visitors to the Moss Rose. Kevin Keegans Fulham amongst others, and of course the visit of Manchester City. One fact that emerged from this year is that when City finished 9th in the inaugural year of the Premiership with an average attendance of 24,698, Macclesfield were 1 point from being relegated from the Conference with crowds of less than 1000. Maybe money isn't everything after all?

Enjoy the book and relive a miracle in Macclesfield.

Paul Atherton
Macclesfield 1998

WHEN Efe Sodje rose above the Torquay defence to head home Macclesfield's first ever Football League goal, it heralded their arrival in the big time after a titanic four year struggle.

That single moment on the opening day of the season seemed to transgress mere sporting achievement. It was a goal laced with pure emotion not only for the fans but for the entire town.

This isn't a tale of success bought by a rich 'Jack Walker' benefactor. It's a story of glory founded on spirit, selfless determination and heart-wrenching hard work from everybody connected with the club.

Against all odds, despite every setback imaginable, Macclesfield Town were finally taking on the big boys and beating them hands down.

The scale of this achievement should certainly not be underestimated. In the four years prior to promotion Macc had overcome the tragic deaths of both Chairman and Vice-Chairman, rejection by the Football League after winning the Conference in 1995, a financial crisis which rocked the very heart of the club and a cash shortage with severely tested the powers of boss Sammy McIlroy.

And to cap it all, only days before the Torquay match, Macc were served with a high court writ demanding over £500,000 which threatened the very existence of the club.

Macclesfield Town should have been buried in the non-league Pyramid system and not scaling it's peak in such a glorious fashion.

That first game against Torquay was a huge relief. Many of us spent the entire 90 minutes pinching ourselves, reflecting on past traumas and soaking up the atmosphere of the occasion. It was one of those moments in life when you only actually believe something is occurring when you witness it with your own eyes.

At one point I began reflecting on how Macclesfield had got to this stage. When had the spark which propelled Macc into Division Three truly ignited?

Numerous incidents sprang to mind, like the first Conference title win, the FA Trophy victory at Wembley or the moment Sammy McIlroy walked into Moss Rose after, ironically, being second choice for the job after Mike McKenzie.

But I came to the conclusion that Macc's triumph was borne out of the embers of the final game of the 1992/93 season. Macc were only 90 minutes away from returning to the Northern Premier League. The only way they could avoid the drop was by gaining a result at Wycombe Wanderers who were already crowned Conference champions. As the final whistle sounded, Macc had somehow scraped out a fabulous one-nil victory, courtesy of a strike from big centre-forward Roy Green. Macclesfield had been saved and there was only one way to go - onward and upward.

Peter Wragg's inevitable reward was the sack but he had already taken his place in the Moss Rose history books after a string of successful achievements at the helm. It was, after all, Wragg who had lifted the Silkmen into the Conference. But it was undoubtedly the right decision, Wragg's day had gone and it was time for a change.

The man chosen to rebuild the Silkmen was Sammy McIlroy MBE, although doubts were raised at the time about his non-league pedigree. But it represented an inspired change of direction at the club.

Here was a man who had achieved almost everything as a player. The 'Last of the Busby Babes' was a folk hero at Old Trafford. A man who had played for and learnt from the likes of Sir Matt Busby, Tommy Docherty and Billy Bingham. He had been capped over 80 times by his country and was a member of the famous side which beat Spain in their own backyard during the 1982 World Cup. Quite simply the biggest name Macc had ever picked for the hotseat.

But despite his credentials, McIlroy had endured a tortuous start in management. He began at Northwich Victoria where he first linked up with assistant boss Gil Prescott.

The duo didn't last long at Drill Field and after a disagreement with the chairman, they left the club. McIlroy moved to lowly Ashton as he continued his managerial apprenticeship. He did well but had no hesitation in successfully applying for the Macclesfield job.

McIlroy knew what he wanted to do from day one and began transforming the side. He knew the type of players he needed, not non-league campaigners but youngsters who had only narrowly failed to make the grade in the Football League. With little money at his disposal McIlroy began to wheel and deal in a manner

Introduction
BY DAVID LAFFERTY

which would have been completely alien to a man who had grown up in the lavish surroundings of Old Trafford.

His reign as boss began disastrously with a heavy defeat at Bath on the opening day of the 1993/94 season and those who'd witnessed the match would have been labelled mad if they'd said Macc would be in Division Three within four years.

But it rapidly turned into a good season and remarkable progress had been made. Both the Drinkwise and Staffordshire Senior Cups were secured. Within nine months McIlroy had transformed a struggling side lacking in belief and ambition into an outfit with genuine hopes of winning the Conference for the first time in their history.

But even this seventh place finish failed to prepare us for what was to occur during the following season. To say everybody was caught on the hop is certainly an understatement.

Arthur Jones had succeeded Alan Brocklehurst as Chairman and he endured a tough introduction to the trials of running a football club. Macc were blazing the trail in the Conference. McIlroy had his supremely confident side ticking like a well-oiled machine.

It slowly began to dawn on the town that here was a side who could win the Conference and reach the Football League.

But there was one major problem which ultimately led to despair. The Moss Rose ground wasn't considered good enough by the Football League.

Officials were still smarting from the mid-season demise of Conference winners Maidstone United and had introduced a set of stringent rules governing admission to the Football League.

The main stumbling block for Macc was the ground had to have a minimum capacity of 6,000 with a certain number of seats ready in time for December 31 in order to qualify for admittance the following season. It was a ridiculous rule which served only to preserve the flagging ships in the lower reaches of the Third Division. In short the League were making it as difficult as possible for Conference sides to achieve the very essence of football - progression.

Almost everyone, barring the Football League, believed that as long as the ground was ready in time for the first game of the following campaign, there should be no reason to prohibit any club from admittance.

Sure enough, despite staunch efforts from directors, Macclesfield Town failed to gain the League's coveted 'A' grading for their ground by the December 31 deadline and the club were left with a huge fight on their hands.

The playing side almost seemed to take a back seat as Macc romped clear of the chasing pack by February and the bookies stopped taking bets on the outcome of the Conference.

With the title seemingly sewn up, the main aim now was to try and persuade the Football League to change their minds. Delegations involving Arthur Jones and Macclesfield's MP Nicholas Winterton visited the Sports Minister and received a sympathetic hearing. But not even government support, strong editorials in local and national newspapers or widespread condemnation from supporters across the land could budge the stubborn men in their Lytham St.Annes Ivory Tower.

Ideas of a ground share with Chester City, who had played at Moss Rose for two season during the eighties, were dismissed by the League whose rules stated that teams could not host home matches outside their immediate conurbation. It didn't seem to trouble them that at the same time they were preventing Macc moving temporarily to Chester, Bristol Rovers' were playing at Bath City which unless I'm mistaken is not in the Bristol conurbation.

The question of whether Macclesfield would gain promotion was the talk of every pub in the town but despite everyone's eternal optimism and willingness to fight on, it was apparent Macc would be going nowhere.

And this sudden realisation that their dreams would not be fulfilled seemed inevitably to reach the players. Despite a huge lead with only two months remaining, Macc's form took a turn for the worse while main rivals Woking began to sense possible glory as McIlroy's men began to flounder.

But despite a number of late scares, McIlroy and Prescott were watching the reserves at their first managerial haunt Northwich Victoria when they heard Woking had lost a crucial match and Macc were champions.

The celebrations lasted long into the night but were inevitably tinged with sadness, frustration and anger. Arthur Jones later called it one of the proudest but saddest days of his life. It was a bitter blow for a club who had come so far only two seasons after escaping relegation.

It'd been hard enough to win the Conference title once, repeating the feat would be doubly difficult. The controversy continued throughout the close season but when the Third Division fixture list was published and Macc weren't included, the fight was clearly over. McIlroy to his credit just got his head down and worked hard to improve his side for another assault on the title.

The first aim of the 1995/96 season was to avoid a repeat of the previous campaign and get the ground up to scratch, a task approached with renewed zeal by Arthur Jones and his board. The team were faring well on the field but it was apparent early on that Macc would not have things all their own way. Stevenage, complete with Efe Sodje and Barry Hayles, were looking like the side to beat from an early stage.

But the club ploughed on and Jones provided funding to rebuild the Silkmen terrace, erect a temporary stand and generally get the ground up to scratch.

With only days to spare before the December 31 deadline, the terracing was completed and Macc had ensured their eligibility for the Football League.

It was a great occasion but this season was also destined to be tinged with sadness. Bob Isherwood had become Arthur Jones' vice-chairman, sharing a lot of the workload and a genuine love for the club. Jones had found someone who shared his

passions and the pair were forming a successful partnership when tragedy struck.

In February, Isherwood collapsed and died shortly after selling his car business to devote more time to his family and his club. Jones was distraught. It truly seemed that someone, somewhere was testing the metal of Macclesfield Town to the limit. The funeral was an emotional occasion but Jones vowed to carry on and fulfill his and Bob's dreams.

They say the Conference is the hardest league to get out of and in Macc's case it was certainly living up to its reputation. Macc were posting some decent results but were unable to sustain a serious title challenge. They finished fourth behind champions Stevenage who were also denied entry to Division Three, a decision which they took to the courts.

But as the title dreams faded, Macc had slowly but surely been edging their way towards a return to the hallowed Wembley turf after a superb FA Trophy run. It was a glorious 'Wembley' day which will live long in the memory and one man was certainly cherishing the occasion.

Arthur Jones had been, above all else, a football fan. He had played at a decent level in his youth and like the rest of us had dreamt that one day he'd be lacing his boots in the shadows of the famous Twin Towers. Instead of boarding the bus with the rest of the directors, Arthur took his place alongside the players at the front of their coach for the drive through the fans to the ground. He loved every minute of it and the sight of Arthur sprinting his way to the pre-match

official banquet after running slightly late was said to be one of the more enduring memories of the day. He told people that in contrast to 12 months earlier, this was one of the proudest days of his life to be the chairman of a side in a Wembley final. Little did anyone know that less than four months later he would tragically take his own life alone in his back street offices. But on that day at least he was the happiest man on the planet.

Tony Hemmings scored one of the finest goals witnessed at Wembley to seal the Trophy for the Silkmen. Macc had turned a difficult campaign into a triumphant success.

McIlroy enjoyed his day but was already planning for the following season. He knew his present team hadn't been good enough to lift the title and with Kidderminster and Stevenage looking strong he had a huge job on his hands to wrest back the title.

The 1996/97 season began well. Macc lost only one match from their first 11 games and the lowest they reached was fourth place. The team were playing well, 1723 turned up at Moss Rose against Stevenage and there was a genuine belief that McIlroy's team strengthening was producing dividends. Everything in Macclesfield's garden was well and truly rosy.

Which made the events of September even harder to comprehend. I can still remember the day vividly.

I received a call at the Express office at around 9.30am. Arthur Jones had been found dead in his Roe Street office with a gun by his side. Initially, it seemed highly improbable but slowly it sank in that it must be true however absurd it appeared at the time.

Arthur Jones was a seemingly successful man on the face of things. He had a thriving business with all the material trappings of success. A Jaguar, big house, big cigars and a manner which oozed class and distinction. But the facts of the matter were that he had taken his own life.

Everyone was baffled in the aftermath of Arthur's death. He had given no indication that he was in any trouble of any sort. No note was ever found.

It later transpired that Arthur's business was in serious trouble. He was in the notoriously risky commodities broking business. He was a fiercely proud man and the public humiliation of losing his business had obviously become too much to bear. Sammy McIlroy was distraught, Arthur had become a kind of father figure to him. He was moved to say: 'I've lost more than a chairman, I've lost a personal friend. I said after Matt Busby there would never be another man like him and there'll never be another man like Arthur Jones.'

The ramifications of Arthur's sudden death were serious for Macclesfield Town. It was mainly Arthur's money which had propelled the Silkmen to the lofty position they now found themselves in.

Whenever he was asked for money Arthur was said to have produced his chequebook. The issue of whether it was his own personal cash or capital from his business is still being fiercely argued over by lawyers at the time of writing.

It was a desperate time at Moss Rose. The one man who was paying

the bills was no longer there. There were serious fears that the club would go out of existence with long term commitments the Silkmen would struggle to meet.

The club were forced to pass buckets around the crowd to raise £6,000 to pay for striker Carwyn Williams who had been bought shortly before Jones' death. Appeals were made for people to come forward and invest in the club which was being run by the remaining board members without a Chairman. The people of the town were asked to turn out in bigger numbers to help the club's bid for survival. It seemed for a time that the unthinkable could occur and Macclesfield Town would either have to sell all their players or go out of business.

On the pitch the team's performances were seemingly unaffected by the chairman's death. If anything it seemed to spur them on, they wanted to win the title as a tribute to Arthur Jones.

But by mid-November, despite being seemingly handily positioned in second-place, the Silkmen were 15 points behind runaway leaders Kidderminster who looked unbeatable. The bookies stopped taking bets and the creditors of Arthur Jones company stated their intention to come knocking on the doors of Moss Rose. It was one of the lowest points in the history of the Silkmen.

Hopes that everything had been rescued were raised in December when supposed saviour Michael Syer joined the board promising to revitalise the club's commercial activities. But this proved short-lived and Syer left the

club after a brief but eventful stay.

Alan Cash was voted in as club chairman with a mandate to keep the club afloat. A share issue was launched through the Macclesfield Express which produced a tremendous response from the fans. It was this money in the main which saw the club through until the end of the season. The efforts of the remaining directors during this period should certainly not be underestimated. It was the most trying of times. But the strength of Cash and directors such as John Brooks and Roy Higginbotham kept the club on course in the choppiest of waters.

Slowly but surely the mood of optimism was coming back to the club. The players were performing superbly, boosted by the arrival of midfielder Chris Byrne who literally burst onto the scene with a hat-trick inside 30 minutes of his full debut.

By the end of December the gap between Macc and Kidderminster had narrowed to only seven points. By January it was down to only two points and the race was well and truly on with Stevenage also mounting a serious challenge. All this while McIlroy was forced to trim his squad to cut the wage bill.

On March 1 the Silkmen finally hit top spot for the first time in the season. They were simply unstoppable. Since losing 1-0 at home to Kidderminster on December 10, Macc had won eight of their nine games to gain pole position. Their fine form continued throughout March but they still couldn't shake off their two rivals.

Matters came to a head during a tremendous match against Stevenage on March 29 which summed up the spirit of the club. It was a match both teams had to win to stand any chance of lifting the title.

But the game was going badly. Macc were two-nil down and John Askey had been sent-off with 37 minutes remaining.

Unbelievably, against all odds, Steve Wood pulled one back then shortly afterwards Carwyn Williams levelled from the spot. And with only minutes remaining, Wood sent a 25 yard free-kick into the back of the net. As the final whistle went the scenes at Broadhall Way were unforgettable. Macc fans began to sense that after all the turmoil of the previous four years, glory was within their grasp. It was said that Stevenage manager Paul Fairclough was so drained by the afternoon that he went to bed at 7pm that evening.

But two days later yet another setback hit the club, the team were brought down to earth with a bang losing 4-1 at Hednesford. There was still plenty of work to do. Two wins and a draw however during April meant that if Macc won at relegation threatened Halifax in the penultimate game of the season then the title was theirs.

It was an agonising match. Macc started brilliantly, going two nil up after only 26 minutes. McIlroy had one hand firmly clasped on the trophy. Halifax pulled one back before the break but Peter Davenport restored Macc's two goal advantage in the 79th minute. Only 11 minutes stood between Macc and the Third Division. But after all they'd been through we should have known it wouldn't have

been as simple as that. In the 81st minute Kevin Horsfield hit the Shaymen's second and then of all people former Macc player Kevin Hulme forced home an equaliser with time fast running out.

The game finished 3-3 and McIlroy was deflated.

He now had to raise his side for the final game of the season at Kettering which they had to win to secure the title or hope Kidderminster lost at Gateshead. The build-up to the biggest game in the club's history was tense, and yet again the club were struck by the hoodoo which seemed determined to bring the club to it's knees. Player-of-the-year Steve Payne, a hugely influential centre-half, was struck down on the eve of the game with appendicitis. It was another bitter blow.

McIlroy shuffled his pack but the 1500 travelling fans feared the worst when Kettering took the lead after only seven minutes. But that was the signal for the Chris Byrne show to begin. 'Goldenboots' headed his first after 11 minutes, hammered home his second from 30 yards then sealed his hat-trick shortly after the half-hour mark. At half-time Macc were 3-1 ahead and Kidderminster were losing to Gateshead.

At last there was light at the end of the tunnel and Macc duly won 4-1 to finally receive their just reward of winning the Conference title and reaching the Third Division.

The celebrations lasted long into the night and McIlroy and the fans paid tribute to Arthur Jones and reflected on the scale of their achievement. It was a momentous day

and no-one would have begrudged the club their success.

The summer months passed by quickly but with no major backers coming forward, McIlroy realised that he would again have little money to spend in comparison to the Football League fatcats of Peterborough and Notts County they were about to encounter. The club were about to embark on another huge struggle.

Then Efe Sodje rose above the Torquay defence to head home Macc's first ever Football League goal and set up the most amazing season in the history of Macclesfield Town Football Club.

David Lafferty
Sports Editor - Macclesfield Express

August

WHERE had our end of season break gone? It seemed only ninety minutes since we had mopped the sweat from our brows and collected the Vauxhall Conference trophy back in May. From the moment the final whistle went on that historic occasion at Kettering the football club set in motion a chain of events that would change the face of Macclesfield Town F.C. for ever.

The decision was made to give all the lads who had played a part in gaining promotion the opportunity to turn full time.

Many thought the opportunity was too good to pass up, whilst some believed the risk of a career change at this stage of their lives too great. The management team had to bring in new faces, but so did the other ninety one teams in the professional ranks, the majority of which were able to draw on healthier resources.

Some players were unable to commence the full time training regime as they had to work the notice given to their employers. A suitable training ground was needed, pre-season friendlies had to be organised, dozens of trialists had to be considered, fitness levels improved, team selection finalised, all with a focal point of August 9th and the historic opening fixture against Torquay United.

When the match with Torquay finally arrived on that sweltering day in August, it brought with it a host of national media coverage. We had a high profile manager and were the first team for four seasons to gain promotion from the Vauxhall Conference. Whether we enjoyed success or endured failure the media were going to report it. Our usual match preparations were interrupted as one person or another had to be excused for interviews. Everywhere we turned there seemed to be microphones and cameras. There were a few nervous players in the dressing room that day, and as the three and a half thousand supporters came through the turnstiles, we knew we had high expectations to live up to. We couldn't stand the heat in the dressing room any more and eventually, the referee called both teams onto the pitch. After the disappointment of being denied promotion when winning the Conference title in 1995, nine months hard slog last season to win the league for the second time in three years, two months of hard pre-season training and countless hours of work put in by everybody connected with the club, Andy Mason tapped the ball to Richard Landon to kick off a whole new exciting chapter in the life of Macclesfield Town.

Team spirit over recent seasons had played as important a part in our success as anything else, and new players had to fit in, both on and off the pitch. It took one of those players, Efe Sodje, only six minutes to convince any of his doubters that his heart was with his new club by scoring our first goal in the Football League. Torquay equalised and could have had another before Richard Landon scored the winner to put our first three points on the table. However, little did we know that we had just beaten one of the teams that were going to be right up there in the promotion shake up.

After the match, there was a certain amount of sympathy shown towards the Torquay players as there was a feeling that a victory was always going to be ours. There wasn't the normal feeling associated with a football match before the game, more a sense of occasion. It was our party and the three thousand Silkmen who turned up were not going to let Torquay spoil it. We got through that match on adrenaline, and despite riding our luck at times, gained a belief in ourselves that come the end of the season, we would not be involved in a relegation battle.

Our first away fixture in the football league appeared a particularly difficult prospect. Brighton were also very much in the spotlight due to boardroom unrest, and after a late run last season to avoid relegation they were being tipped for promotion. They were playing their first 'home' game of the season and the highly charged atmosphere was due mainly to the tensions between their fans and the board of directors. The game ended one-all, a result that we would have settled for before the game. I hit the bar with a header in injury time but was not overly concerned. Three points would have been nice but it wouldn't be long until we get our first away win!

Doncaster were the next visitors to the Moss. Following the Brighton game, it was a coincidence that they too had an axe to grind with their board of directors. After our well publicised difficulties last season when many were predicting we would go out of business, it was ironic we now appeared to be one of the more stable clubs in the league.

Doncaster, even at this early stage in the season, were favourites for relegation. One of their fans ran on to the pitch to vent his anger at his club. A pitch invasion is often looked on as humorous to the average fan and there are always cheers as the stewards or police chase and fail to catch the intruder. As a player, however, it can sometimes be quite disrupting. If you have your opposition under heavy pressure when the incident occurs, they have a couple of minutes to get their breath back and regroup which they wouldn't normally. It was immaterial against Doncaster as we were by far the superior team, but in a tighter encounter where one goal is needed to win the match it may not appear as funny. We jumped to the top of the table after this victory and were still unbeaten. This third division lark appeared easy!

*Professional football means full-time training, secluded training grounds and high levels of security. Not in Division Three.
Still one out of three is a start!*

Unsurprisingly,a massive media circus persuades the mayor to visit The Moss Rose.But will he be seen again?

A moment that many thought they would never see.....

Efe Sodje carves his name in history.

.......and cannot contain his delight.

League goals are like buses, much to the delight of the Moss Rose faithful.Richard Landon and Andy Mason celebrate the winner against Torquay.

The League's newest manager explains a winning start.

The splendour of Brighton's temporary Priestfield home is the setting for the first away game.

A great late save by Ryan Price sees the Silkmen gain a one all draw to remain unbeaten!

The visit of Doncaster Rovers brings with it an unacceptable face of football - Ken Richardson, the shady looking gentleman takes refuge in the dugout.

In spite of the fracas off the pitch things continue as normal on it as another home win is secured John Askey nods in from the far post.

Who said a referee has the toughest job in football?

Andy Mason soars skywards to win a header at Hartlepool.

September

WE came through the first few games of our campaign on hype and adrenaline. It was now we would have to dig in and work hard and get results by out performing the opposition. We had the impression teams didn't want to be beaten by us because we were still seen in their eyes as non-leaguers and consequently they would just find that little bit of extra effort from somewhere.

After our bright start to the season, the visit to Rochdale brought us down to earth with a bump. We believed ourselves to be the better footballers, but after a tidy opening start we were bulldozed by a physically stronger side. Rochdale opened up a two goal lead and then prevented us from seriously threatening their goal. Following our first defeat, we knew the season was going to be a long one and we weren't going to have things all our own way. We had to earn the right to play football. If we matched sides physically, our footballing ability would always bring us out on top. This was what was being preached to us all week during training sessions. We had two home games coming up and a lot of people to whom we owed a performance - not least the very encouraging support that travelled to the Rochdale game.

Many were predicting an end to our competent start to the season after slipping to tenth in the league. Darlington were our next opponents and took an early lead at the Moss. If there were any doubts as to our ability they should appear now. Two Phil Power goals, however, restored our self confidence and gained us three more points. This was quickly followed by a three nil home victory over Jan Molby's highly fancied Swansea City and we were hoisted into second place in the league.

These two home victories, however, were not without their negative aspects. The two Steves, Wood and Payne, were both injured. We always knew that a crippling injury list would considerably affect our season, but believed we would be able to get by with a relatively light one. Another defeat, the second of the season, this time at Scarborough, and another injury to another Steve, this time Hitchen, prompted the management to dip into the transfer market. To buy proven football league players was an option, but very often their financial demands were just too high. The manger decided instead on a loan signing, so Mark Cooper was drafted in from Hartlepool United.

The defeat against Scarborough was one we wanted to get out of our system straight away. Unfortunately with no midweek fixture we had to wait until the following weekend before we were able to get rid of our frustrations. A midweek game is one the players look forward to. If it comes on the heels of a victory you just want to keep the bandwagon rolling on. If it comes after a defeat you want to put your errors right immediately. On this occasion, though, the next game was the visit of high flying, big spending Peterborough. This was just the kind of game we had been looking forward to playing all last season.

Peterborough and ourselves were both in the top six and a crowd of over 3000 witnessed a great game. A 1-1 scoreline, we emerged with our reputations intact which was important to the players after the Scarborough defeat. The season was just beginning to take shape. We weren't playing on adrenaline anymore. We were knuckling down to some hard work and playing attractive football. It appeared that we weren't going to struggle to stay in the league. In our pre-season target of avoiding relegation, we were perhaps underestimating ourselves. We could finish midway up this league, with an outside chance of a play off position. If we were going to achieve this we had to start winning games away from the Moss.

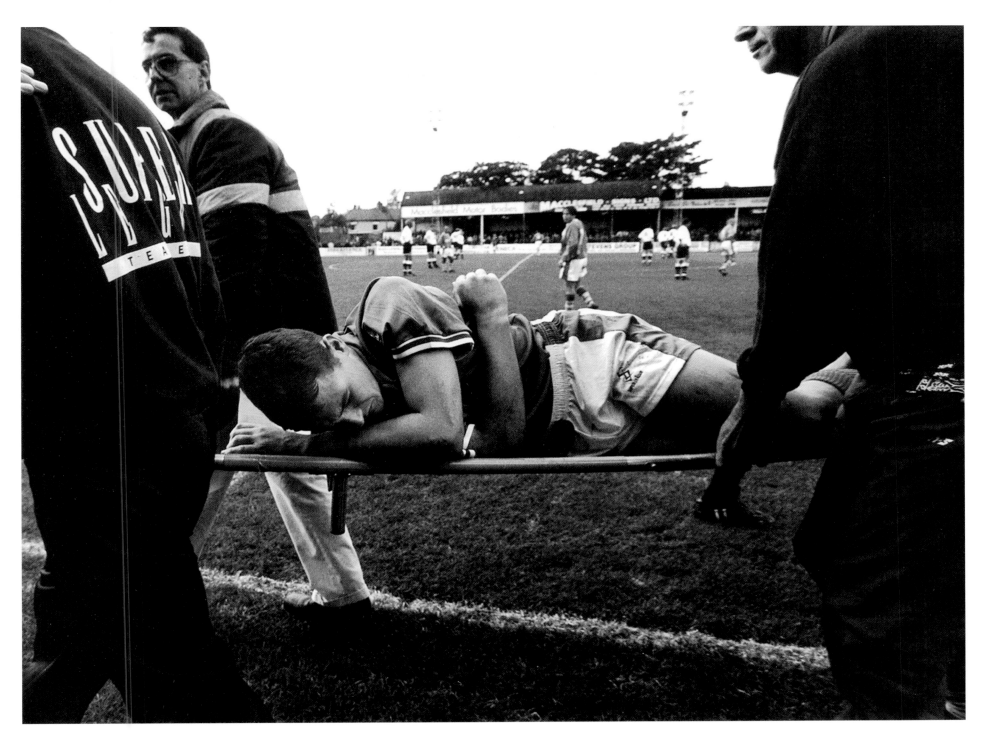

Payne in pain - Steve is stretchered off with an ankle injury.

Barry Fry laughs off Alan Cash's suggestion that Macclesfield will win promotion, while Peterborough won't even make the play off's.

Another chance goes begging.

Darren Tinson needs to work on his backhand.

The hand of Sodje!...with the World Cup in France coming up, Efe Sodje tries to attract the eye of the Nigerian selectors with his own version of famous World Cup moments.

October

AN away journey to a strong Leyton Orient side was the second of a three game run against potential promotion contenders. A draw would normally be seen as a respectable result, but with the media picking up on our inability to win away from home, a victory was what the players and management were after.

Richard Landon again came off the bench to score a late equaliser to continue his impressive goals per game ratio. Just like the Peterborough match, we equalised very late in the game. Was this a sign of our superior fitness? The belief amongst the players was that there was no fitter team in the league. One of the most important moves by the club was to bring in a fitness coach. Peter Everson set out a programme the players were to follow from the very first weeks of pre-season training back in July that would bring us to the peak of our fitness for the start of the season. His warm up routines were followed religiously before every training session and match and his enthusiasm and motivation has certainly played an important part in the success of our first season in the league.

The final game of the three was perhaps our sternest test. Notts County are the oldest club in the Football League and they were playing host to the newest, a point not missed by the media as they again come out in force to witness this special occasion. Would they be congratulating us on our first away victory or would the headlines be that we had failed to win away from home again and still had a lot to learn in this division?

As it happened, we produced just about our finest performance of the season, either home or away. Some of the football produced in the second half in the fantastic Meadow Lane stadium would not have looked out of place across the River Trent on The City Ground, home of Nottingham Forest. Unfortunately we were unable to turn our superiority into the victory we were still searching for, so had to settle for another 1-1 draw. But if we could keep turning performances out like this one, we would certainly win a lot more games than we would lose.

We now had a home game with Mansfield coming up followed by another home game with Exeter. The way our home form was going there was no reason why we wouldn't be able to win both games and strengthen our position in the top half of the table. The players were coming round to the way of thinking that we were a very difficult team to get anything from on our home ground. If we were able to keep that as a foundation for building on, an average away record would put us well up towards the play off places.

The Mansfield and Exeter games reaped four points and nearly six thousand fans streamed through the turnstiles for those two games.

This was especially pleasing to the players as it showed there was a belief in our ability from the townsfolk of Macclesfield. We were rewarding the supporters who visited the Moss regularly with good football and results to match. How long would it be until we were giving the same value for money away from home? Chester, our local derby this season, would be the ideal place to pick up our first three points on our travels.

We entered the Chester game in sixth position. Chester were also enjoying a successful spell, were unbeaten in the league at home and although we still hadn't won away from home, we had only lost twice on our travels. The success the lads have had over recent seasons had left us with a belief in ourselves that we were a very difficult side to beat. As ever, we entered the match with Chester full of confidence and when the clock was ticking down and we were leading courtesy of a Richard Landon goal, we felt fairly assured of gaining our first away win of the season. However, a thirty yard wonder strike that flew past a disbelieving Ryan Price, earned Chester a share of the spoils.

At the end of October our away record showed that we had drawn five of our seven games and lost the other two. At first glance it was a pretty respectable record. But with three points for a win we would have been higher than our eighth place in the league if we had won two and lost five of those away games! In the Chester dressing room after the game, I believe the first serious concerns surfaced about our inability to win an away game. We were performing well and were not getting beaten but we needed to start winning soon if we were to have a real crack at getting into the play offs.

The Moss Rose subbuteo style.

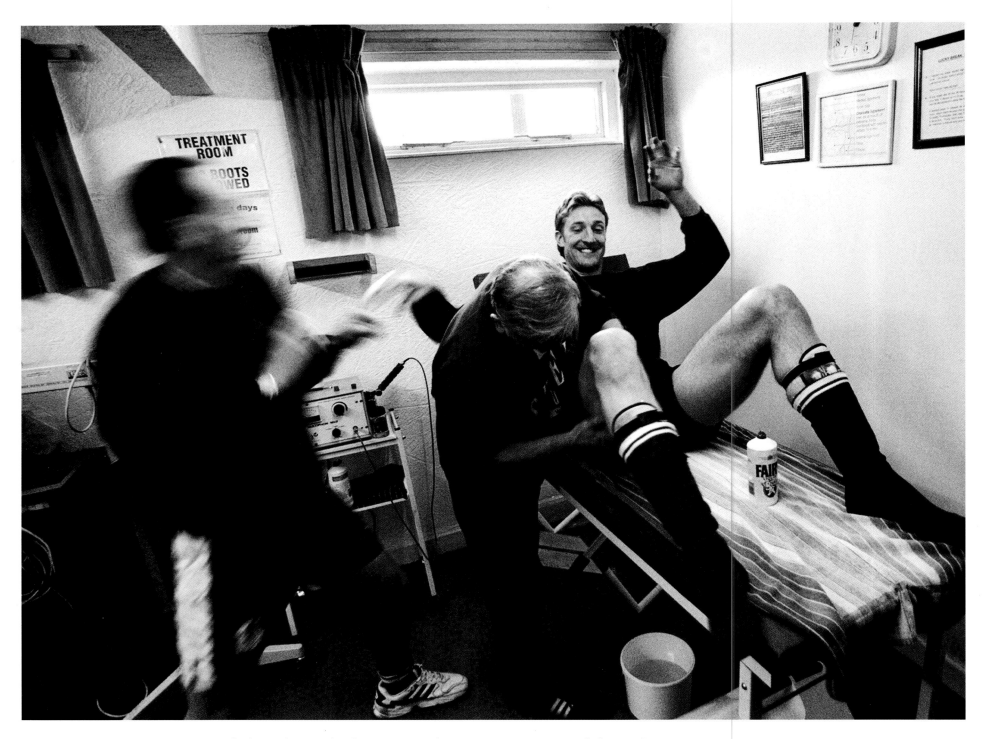

Ec finds another use for the Fairy Liquid on Ryan Price - Steve Wade beats a hasty retreat!

A gleeful fan proudly informs the visiting support of the score. A thoughtful act as The Moss Rose isn't equipped with an electronic scoreboard.

With a rise in admission prices this season, one fan finds the hole in the fence the best way to see the game and still keep all of his pocket money.

Darren Tinson respects the wishes of the ground staff.

November

NOVEMBER is the month of the first round of the F.A.Cup. The average Vauxhall Conference team has to play four rounds before they even reach the first round proper. This season, many of the lads had reached further than ever before without even having played a game. The club was only two wins away from a potentially massive money making game against one of the Premiership big boys. The draw was made and we were left with a not too particularly mouth watering tie against Hartlepool United at their Victoria ground.

Before the tie was to be played there were three very important league games to tackle. The first two were very disappointing encounters with us not scoring and gaining only one point. We had only one game left before the cup tie and a win was needed to boost the teams confidence.

The result and performance, a three one home victory over Cambridge, was just the shot in the arm we needed if we were to get anything out of the cup tie and progress into further rounds.

Preparations during the week were hampered due to the adverse weather conditions. Much of the training had to be done indoors with Diane, the clubs administration manager, under strict orders from the management to telephone the players and instruct us to bring our indoor footwear to train in. Sure enough the only person to forget their training shoes was the person who had placed the order in the first place! Watching the gaffa trying to wear his football boots on the hard gym floor we were training on got the lads in just the

relaxed frame of mind we needed for our arduous game at Hartlepool.

An extremely hard fought encounter was fully expected and the Hartlepool side certainly didn't disappoint. In fact, they appeared to be too wound up as they had a man sent off in the first half. With us leading by a goal and playing against ten men one could be forgiven for thinking we would sail through to the second round. However, a mixture of the spirit of the north east and the tradition of the F.A. Cup throwing up its own typical surprises left us trailing 2-1 with had clock ticking away. Our own spirit which has been of paramount importance over recent seasons was not left wanting when it was called upon and we raced into a four three lead. A world class save by Ryan Price in the dying minutes preserved our lead, and when the final whistle blew seconds later, who could blame us for dreaming about what may be in the further rounds. Little were we to know that our dreams were going to turn into our worst nightmares!

The following two league games pretty much followed the way the season was unfolding. An away defeat against Shrewsbury and a home victory over Hull left us just outside the all important top seven places and had the press congratulating us on our wonderful home record but slating us for our dismal away record. Why couldn't that last minute header at Brighton have just sneaked under the bar instead of hitting it? A victory in our first away game of the season would have made life a lot easier for us. We had a monkey on our back and there was only one way to get rid of it.

We were trying our best but the luck was just not with us.

Lincoln was our next visit, not an enviable task when they were top of the league and with our away record. John Beck's side are always difficult to beat and there is inevitably an intimidatory atmosphere. We overcame all the pressures with a first half performance that left us bewildered as to how we were only leading by a single Stuart Whittaker goal. The second half was a bruising encounter and we were unable to hang on to our lead. Normally to come away from the table toppers with a point would be a satisfactory result. However, with our away record we were not in a normal situation therefore we left the impressive Sincil Bank stadium disappointed.

High fives all around as Neil Sorvel takes the field - the bandana slowly replaces the bobble hat at Macc.

"I remember when the football was crap, I could count the crowd on one hand, and the players wore those nice figure hugging shorts!"
Who says things were better in the old days?

Another perfect 10 - another home win.

The Moss Rose time warp takes us back to 1960. Even then kids refused to pay to watch the Cheshire Senior Cup matches.

Training moves to Kings School playing fields. How many other professional clubs have to use rugby posts instead of goal posts?

December

THE game that the players had one eye on since the draw for the second round of the F.A Cup was made had finally arrived. Walsall were the club that had been pulled out of the hat directly after us, and so, on December 6th, they would be making the relatively short journey northwards to the Moss.

Once the draw had been made, there was a strong feeling of anticipation floating around the club. We knew we had a very real possibility of making the third round which is of course when all the First Division and Premier League sides enter. Although Walsall were playing their league football in one division higher than ours, a quick glance at their away record showed they were still to record a victory on their travels, an encouraging sign for a team with our unblemished home record. There is a special atmosphere around football clubs on F.A Cup days, and as kick off time approached, one could almost cut the air with a pair of scissors. Little were we to know, however, that we were in for the most embarrassing ninety minutes of our careers.

Two Frenchmen, Boli and Peron, provided the flair to complement the workrate and application of the rest of the excellent Walsall team, and they destroyed us with an exhibition of first class passing, moving and exhilarating finishing. Efe Sodje was dismissed for a foul early in the second half, and as the resulting penalty kick was calmly slotted away, the remaining players on the pitch couldn't help but look with a degree of envy as he trudged off the field. With the scoreline reading four goals to nil, the remaining thirty minutes or so were going to be the longest of our lives.

In the cold light of day, the seven nil scoreline appeared a thousand times worse than it had the night before. The several inquests that followed that week were all clouded in an air of disbelief as to what had actually taken place. How could we have been beaten 7-0? We travelled to Barnet for our next league game and finished on the wrong end of a 3-1 scoreline. We were still shell-shocked from the previous week's encounter. Unless we came to terms with it quickly, our season was going to be over by Christmas.

The defeat at Barnet had left us thirteenth in the league, the lowest position we had been in all season. With three games to be played over the next eight days, we would have a much more realistic picture of what our targets should be for the remainder of the season. A hard fought 1-0 home victory over Cardiff was noted for the bravery of Steve Wood who played with a protective mask covering his second broken cheekbone of the season. It was his goal that provided us with the much needed win, but this was followed up with a demoralising defeat against Darlington on Boxing Day. We were midway through the season and were lying halfway up the table. If we had been offered this position at the start of the season we would definitely have taken it. However, our expectations had changed since then and we knew we were good enough to mount a serious challenge for a play off spot. We just had to find a little more consistency, and that would only occur if we started to pick up wins away from home.

Rochdale were the next visitors to the Moss, and the game was seriously in doubt due to the heavy rain that was lying on the playing surface. If the game was to go ahead the conditions were going to be atrocious. It was touch and go right up until three'o'clock, but thankfully the rain eased enabling the game to be played.

Martin McDonald received the man of the match award for his never say die performance and Steve Wood again played in his protective mask. We were victorious against a hard-working Rochdale side that had been a bit of a bogey team over us recently. They were a physically strong side who had overpowered us on our last two encounters. On this occasion, though, we more than matched them in the most trying of conditions. Perhaps we had learnt our lesson and had finally got over our torment from the Walsall defeat. If that was the case, were we now better equipped mentally and physically to have a real go over the remaining four months of the season?

Its just one of those days as Walsall put seven past the lads, which is anything but magnificent.

Steve Wood goes to extreme lengths to get free opera tickets.

December 28th - and these Rochdale fans decide to remove their new Christmas knitwear after several derogatory remarks from Bart Simpson in the front row.

Football the 3rd Division way.

Under all that mud is Martin McDonald - probably

January

AT this time of the season many of the games are postponed. One week the pitches are waterlogged, the next frozen over. The home match with Scunthorpe was cancelled at the last possible minute, the visitors and their supporters having already arrived at the ground.

Pete Everson didn't miss the opportunity to take a quick improvised training session on the ice as the manager and Gil were left wondering what might have been.

As we entered the new year, we took the chance to take stock of the previous five months of the season. Lying twelfth in the league was a position we realistically should have been pleased with, but we couldn't help thinking we were better than that.

Unbeaten at home in twelve games, with only three of those drawn indicated we should have been higher in the league. However, it only took a look at our away results to show we needed to make an improvement. It was still tight between the top dozen sides with only Notts County putting together a consistent run to form a gap at the top of the table. There was still a lot to play for as we entered our next away game at fellow promotion hopefuls Torquay.

The preparations were spot on and we stayed overnight in nearby Exeter. There was a mood amongst the players that tomorrow would finally be the day that we would banish our away day blues. When the match came, there was another encouraging following urging us on, but unfortunately we failed to produce the goods again, and everyone left for the long journey home immensely disappointed.

A quick look down the fixture list showed the next away game was against the leagues whipping boys Doncaster Rovers. Surely they would be able to provide us with our first three points on the road, but first we had two home games to concentrate on. If we could pick up maximum points in the games against Hartlepool and Scunthorpe we would be back up close to the play-off positions.

Both games went according to plan, six points and two convincing performances provided a platform for the Doncaster game.

All week, the talk was about Macclesfield surely ending the away drought. The build up of pressure increased as kick-off time approached. On paper this would be the easiest game of the season, but it felt like the most difficult.

Doncaster weren't going to just lie down and let us walk all over them, we had to earn the right to win the game.

The three-nil victory we recorded was the most important of the season since the opening day but ironically it was one of least impressive performances on our travels. There was a collective sigh of relief when the whistle blew and we knew there was no reason why we couldn't start picking up more points away from home. We'd managed to get through our recent sticky patch and were still well in touch with the promotion hopefuls.

Consistency was the key. Other teams around us were beating each other and if we could continue our run of good results we wouldn't be far away from reaching our goal. With the exception of Notts County, who were running away with the title, there wasn't much between the other dozen or so teams involved in the promotion battle. It was time to throw caution to the wind.

What were we afraid of? We had to take the season by the scruff of the neck and put together a run that would take us higher up the league, starting with our next opponents Brighton.

Under new boss Steve Gritt, Brighton had picked up slightly, and they produced one of the better performances seen at the Moss by a visiting side all season. However, we just about edged it in a tight encounter to record our fourth consecutive victory and move into fifth.

If we were to hold onto this position for another four months it would have represented a fantastic achievement.

Looking at our league position, if we didn't get into the play-offs from here we would have an immense feeling of failure.

A quick glance at the following month's fixtures showed February could be the month that would make or break our season, How right that proved to be.

Much to the disappointment of Gil, Peter and Sammy, the home game with Scunthorpe is called off. Groundsheets were laid down too late and the pitch freezes. Sammy shows his frustration claiming "Sometimes we've still got one foot in the Conference"

The turning point? Brighton's Steve Grit congratulates Sammy on a one - nil win that takes us into fifth position

Calm down, I heard you the first time. The John Askey fan club tell Gil to get the beers in - and no white wine spritzers!

Martin McDonald and Phil Power compare cue sizes prior to the Swansea game.

The players and management discuss tactics over pre - match tea and toast. Meanwhile Frank is left to reflect on the price of washing powder.

Swansea ask if they can leave it there for the game.

Steve Wood gets cautioned for the heinous crime of kicking the ball away.

February

HOME games against Scarborough, Leyton Orient and Notts County plus two away matches at Peterborough and Mansfield would show if we were good enough against five of our promotion rivals.

Scarborough, above us in the league on goals scored, were destroyed by a first half performance that was fuelled by our inept display on the east coast earlier in the season. Three goals to the good at half-time, we were able to ease down in the second-half and start thinking about our next opponents.

Leyton Orient were the next on the list to come and try to spoil our unbeaten home record. They were a strong side who never knew when they were beaten, and you certainly knew you had been in a game after playing 90 minutes against them.

Ryan Price had been up all night attending the birth of his daughter, but still managed to turn in a man-of-the-match performance in our one-nil win. To cap Ryan's perfect day, his dad even won the half-time draw!

The first two games of the month had gone exactly according to plan with maximum points taken. However, Peterborough away was going to be a different kettle of fish.

We arrived at the impressive London Road stadium knowing that victory would push us up into second place in the league. Having won six of our last seven games, including the away victory at Doncaster, we felt there was no reason why we couldn't keep this run going. Peterborough were actually in the middle of a confidence crisis that had seen them slump down the league. It was not a bad time to be playing them.

We dominated the game for long spells but Peterborough always looked threatening on the break. At nil-nil it looked as though the game may be heading for stalemate, but backed by another fantastic away following, Stuart Whittaker produced a piece of magic on the left-wing to set up a goalscoring opportunity for John Askey. When called upon, John is very rarely left wanting and with a nod of his head sent us up to second place in the division.

The victory over Peterborough took more out of us than we thought, and we succumbed to a one goal defeat at Mansfield three days later. Although we had the chances to win the game, our overall performance was disappointing, especially when considering how impressive we were at Peterborough the previous weekend. At the heart of the Mansfield engine room was a curly haired character whose influential performance won him the man-of-the-match award. That all round performance obviously struck a note with our management team because we'd be seeing a lot more of a certain Ben Sedgemore later in the season.

As we entered Mansfield's player's lounge, there were a few anxious looks at the teletext screen to see the other results of the night. Confirmation was there that we had remained in second place despite our defeat. Perhaps someone was smiling down on us, and if they were, could they please carry on smiling for just a couple more months!

The final game of February was against champions elect Notts County. With a run of victories that stretched either side of Christmas, they'd proved themselves far and away the best side in the league and had all but been crowned as champions. Top of the league versus the second place team was the match of the day in our division but there was no way we were going to lie down and let their bandwagon roll on.

The large following that County brought with them had seen more victories on their travels than any other club in the country, but the larger support that were urging us on had seen more home victories than any other in Britain. Something had to give, and we were not in awe of our opponents, especially as we thought we had outplayed them at Meadow Lane back in October.

In another impressive home display we more than matched them in every department and inflicted only their fourth defeat of the season.

We had reaffirmed ourselves in the runners-up spot against the best team in the league. You could forget the 'we'll be happy if we stay up' talk and the 'we're now aiming for the play-offs' nonsense. We were second in the league and we were going to get promoted. Nothing else would suffice anymore. If we didn't get promotion now, we would never forgive ourselves.

"Forget the play-offs. I want to be in Maguluf watching the Cup Final, already promoted." Steve Wade plans his summer holidays.

Training continues at Ryles Park School playing field. Just up the road, Man Utd announce their new £10 million training complex. The gap keeps on widening.

1pm - Ready.........

2.30pm - Steady........

5.45pm - GO....... with the exception of Cec Edey, who keeps Frank from his Valentines Day date.

Take that horrible mask off Dad!

Peterborough v Macclesfield and FIFA test the new Robo - Refs.

McDonald, Askey, and Wood celebrate the winning goal at London Road.

With the team on a roll, a good away following travel to Mansfield expecting the run to continue.

Unfortunately it doesn't work out like that. Mansfield win 1 - 0.

Rain fails to dampen the atmosphere as high flying Notts County come to town.

Sammy's off to celebrate the penalty save against Notts County that does justice to the decision and seals a 2 - 0 win.

History in the making. Supporters celebrate rising to 2nd in Division three. What could possibly go wrong?

March

THE countdown to the end of the season was well and truly on. We had eleven games to play and nine weeks in which to play them. There was no chance of fixture congestion as in previous seasons. It was not unusual for us to play five times in eight days with the cup success we had during our Conference days.

This year, we would be able to play our match on the Saturday and gear our training to reach peak condition for the following weekend.

There was no question over our fitness, so we just ticked over day by day without doing anything exceptionally strenuous.

We had a difficult Cambridge side to overcome closely after our victory over Notts County. Neither side was able to master the awful conditions as the wind ran out a comfortable winner in a dull scoreless draw.

There were ten games remaining, five at home, five away. If we could pick up maximum points from our home games we knew that we would only need a couple of points on our travels to ensure promotion.

Our plan didn't exactly go to plan, though, because in the very next match we failed to break down a defiant Rotherham United and we again drew nil-nil.

That was two games on the trot we had not managed to score. Training routines were altered as we placed more emphasis on crossing and shooting exercises. We needed to regain our confidence in front of goal, and if you can beat big Ryan Price regularly in training you can beat any 'keeper in the league.

We carried this philosophy on the long journey to Colchester. We scored a goal which could have won us the match but a dire second-half performance from the usually solid defence handed the points on a plate to the in-form buoyant Colchester side.

Some of the players were getting a little nervous as a quick look at the form guide showed we'd managed only five points from a possible fifteen. A couple of the lads looked through some of the away programmes we'd picked up over the season to see which fixtures our rivals still had to play. Here we found some reassurance as many of them still had to play one another. If they could continue to take points off each other and we could overcome our little hiccup, our promotion charge would be right back on the rails.

After the defeat at Colchester we knew it was essential to win our next game. Although we'd found our next opponents Shrewsbury difficult opposition at Gay Meadow, we had the feeling we were invincible at the Moss.

Sure enough, after a shaky start we again emerged victorious to keep up right up there in the promotion pack and our incredible home record intact.

Our next match was on the best playing surface in the league, Hull's Boothferry Park. Travelling arrangements were made and it was greed that the 'Black Country Boys', namely Ryan Price and Ben Sedgemore, would meet John Askey at the hotel where we were to have our pre-match meal.

As time passed and the rest of the lads were tucking into their chicken and beans, there was still no sign of Pricey and co.

Deep down, we knew everything should be alright as sensible John Askey was with them to supervise, but it was almost time to leave for the ground.

Just as we were trying to persuade centre-half Steve Payne that he would be playing the game in goal, Gil Prescott's mobile phone rang. On the other end was Pricey explaining how they had accidentally missed a turn off and had ended up in Blackpool! We thought they'd obviously mistaken the Tower for Hull's floodlights.

Hull City had struggled all season, and despite having knocked us out of the Coca-Cola Cup back in August, we entered the game as firm favourites. As things turned out, whilst reducing the home team to only one realistic opportunity, we never really looked like scoring ourselves.

This was a disappointing result and it felt all the worse as we walked up the tunnel. A Hull City fan shouted out the scores of our closest rivals and took great pleasure in informing us they'd all won.

As we sat in the dressing room we were dismayed at our shortcomings. Frank started to pass on the scores from his radio. As he went further through the fixtures we realised the Hull fan had been winding us up. Not one of our closest rivals had managed to win!

The contrast in emotions was indescribable. For the second time this season, somebody was looking down and smiling on us.

Entering April, there were six games remaining, two of which were against teams harbouring ambitions of finishing in the three automatic promotion positions themselves. We had a little good fortune at Hull but we had to make sure we wouldn't have to rely on that again!

Gil Prescott "If we win the Cheshire Senior Cup but pick up some injuries, it will be a bad result" It's a bad result. Martin McDonald damages ankle ligaments during the win over Runcorn and will miss the next three games.

Kieron Durkins' debut is over before it's even started.

"I'm sorry love, but this is about as good as it gets" The groom sums up life, marriage and Humberside in one sentence during the nil - nil draw at Boothferry Park, although the bride's quite content to look at Ben Sedgemores legs.

So in ascending order those winning lottery numbers are 3,5,6,10,13,16 and the bonus ball - er ...Andy Mason keeps them guessing.

The boy in the jacket is disgusted as Horace asks - "Alan who?"

April & May

WITH the finishing line well and truly in sight it would take six more big efforts to guarantee a place in the second division. Lincoln were the next visitors to the Moss and if we could manage a victory we could mentally tick them off as promotion rivals.

The game was as important for them as it was for us and they too arrived looking for a vital win.

Both sides had an equally impressive goals against column so we believed that one goal could decide the outcome. Once the game was under way the action was fast and furious with plenty of goalmouth incidents at both ends. The teams were playing for the highest possible stakes, but it would be the eleven who remained the coolest under pressure who would win the game.

At the half-time interval it was still all square. It had been a difficult first-half but we knew the second was going to be an even tougher battle. Just what sort of battle it turned out to be we could never have imagined.

It looked as though we were heading for a scoreless draw until the ball dropped invitingly to Steve Wood six yards out. Although it was struck in the right direction, it didn't appear to have the power to test a good Third Division keeper.

However, the good Third Division 'keeper was sat in the bath contemplating his earlier challenge on Martin McDonald. His replacement was only able to push the ball into the roof of the net. As the Moss Rose erupted, we couldn't help but think Lincoln had paid the ultimate price for their earlier rashness. We on the other hand had moved one step closer to Division Two.

With five games to play and teams around us dropping points, we knew a victory over our next opponents Scunthorpe, would push us ever closer to our goal. They still had an outside chance of making the play-offs, and if it wasn't for a disastrous ten game run midway through the season, would surely have been right up there in the top four or five. We knew the game wasn't going to be easy, but had high hopes of Pricey and co. finding the ground without a hitch.

On Pricey's map, it was only a couple of miles further down the east coast than Blackpool! However, the size of our task was made doubly difficult when we were on the receiving end of a goal of the season contender in the early minutes of the match. Who could blame the massive travelling army for thinking they had seen all this before?

Despite showing plenty of effort, there was something missing that prevented us from getting an equaliser. When the final whistle blew we couldn't believe we had shot ourselves in the foot yet again. Our home performance against Lincoln had got us into a great position only for us to once again slip up on our travels. As we started lapping the pitch on our warm down routine, other scores began filtering through to us. Barnet and Colchester had both lost, Scarborough and Torquay had both only drawn. We had got out of jail yet again.

To be still holding an automatic promotion place after getting beaten again was something we couldn't believe. For the remaining four games

the ball was in our court. We were to make sure we would never have to rely on other teams results again.

There was a real Easter Monday treat in store for the Macclesfield public as Barnet, only one place below us in the league, were the opposition for our 43rd league game of the season. Again, if we could win, we could theoretically cross them off as promotion contenders. Teams must arrive at the Moss wary of our exceptional home record and who could blame them? We had won all but three of the games that had been played here. We knew if we started well against teams here they would often succumb to the pressure we were putting them under.

This was precisely what happened against Barnet. We raced into a two-nil half-time lead and then sat back and cruised through the second-half. We had jumped to second place in the table, and with only three games to go, we were never going to slip up from here.

There was a trip to Cardiff to negotiate before our final home games of the season, and if we could manage three points we would be able to confirm our runners-up spot in front of our home fans the following week. However, our Jeckyll and Hyde performances continued and we left the pitch at half-time trailing by one goal to nil. Emotions were running high as it looked as though we were heading for our eleventh defeat of the season.

We had lost two of our last three away fixtures and had been fortunate to get away with it. There was no way we were going to let that happen again.

We were in control of our own destiny and all we needed was a good kick up the pants. We got that plus a lot more besides and walking out onto the pitch for the second-half our ears were still ringing.

We got an equaliser through Efe Sodje and then it was left to Neil Sorvel to slot home the goal that would all but assure promotion. The scenes in the dressing room after the game were one of the highlights of the season.

Woody, often accused of being a pub player by his mickey taking team-mates, started calling the Third Division a pub league!

The celebrations following our other two away victories were somewhat tarnished because of the teams which we had beaten. Doncaster didn't have a players lounge so we were unable to buy ourselves a drink after the game, whilst Peterborough had a mightily impressive lounge but had forgotten to renew their liquor licence so there was no alcohol available!

It had been a long time since we were able to walk into a visitors players lounge with our heads held high and get ourselves a drink.

We had a good old sing-song on the way home and another couple of drinks as the feeling of finally coming up with goods when it mattered most sank in.

We weren't taking anything for granted and knew we still had one last hurdle to clear but who could begrudge us celebrating only our third away win of the season.

The whole campaign had been one long rollercoaster ride with so many highs and lows. Now, after nine months, all our hopes and dreams rested on a victory over Chester City at Moss Rose. I can remember looking at this fixture at the start of the season and wondering how important it would be. Perhaps Chester would need a win for promotion or we would need one to survive. I didn't dare think that a victory would guarantee a place in the play-offs. But to be three points from confirming our runners-up spot was just unimaginable.

I arrived at the ground on matchday at half past one. To see the size of the queues at that early stage sent goosebumps up my arm. We had travelled so far over recent seasons and achieved so much, but this eclipsed everything else. To be three points from playing Manchester City, Burnley, Millwall and Stoke was beyond our wildest dreams.

We had travelled full circle. Just like the Torquay match, the media were out in force again. Preparations were hampered due to the number of cameras and microphones and interviews being requested. But most importantly, the feeling was there that it was going to be our day again.

On the opening day of the season, 3000 fans didn't let Torquay spoil the occasion. Twice that number were now going to make sure Chester wouldn't either.

However, in typical Macclesfield style, we didn't make it easy for ourselves. Despite Steve Wood and Neil Sorvel putting us into a two goal lead, Chester pulled one back. Phil Power picked up on a defensive error and shot home to send the home fans delirious.

The joy was shortlived though, as Chester once again reduced the deficit. Eleven minutes to go, and I thought the thirty minutes against Walsall following Efe's sending-off seemed to drag on. Eventually though, the referee put the whistle to his lips for the final time and blew to signify the start of a second successive promotion party. We had reached Division Two, unbelievable!

Although the celebrations went on long into the night, we still had one final game to play at Exeter.

The icing on the cake came when Peter Davenport, making only his second appearance of the season, pounced to score his 100th Football League goal. His strike confirmed another away victory and gave us four wins on the bounce. Who could have wished for a more appropriate note on which to finish the season?

After the end of the season, Paul Atherton, David Lafferty and I met to reflect on the previous nine months. None of us had known what to expect entering the season. It really was a case of heading into the unknown. Following our opening day victory over Torquay though, I believed us capable of handling the step up in quality to the Third Division from the Conference and subsequently thought we were never going to get drawn into any relegation battles.

Secretly I was harbouring thoughts of reaching a play-off position but realistically felt as though we were heading for mid-table obscurity. As we entered the new year, we were still lying half-way down the table.

However, in similar style to the previous year, we put together a string of results that transformed our season.

We had gained promotion from the Conference in the face of the most trying of circumstances and made it two promotions in succession.

It's such an exciting time to be connected with the club at the moment. To be playing teams such as Manchester City is not only a dream come true for the players but also the supporters who have been following the Silkmen through their 122 years in non-league scene.

I can honestly say it's been an absolute honour to have played a part in the success the club has enjoyed in recent years. Who knows what the next chapter will be in the rise and rise of Macclesfield Town FC?

Roary takes the field and makes his way to greet the Lincoln supporters.

Nutmegged! Martin McDonald slips the ball past the Lincoln defence.

1

2

3

4

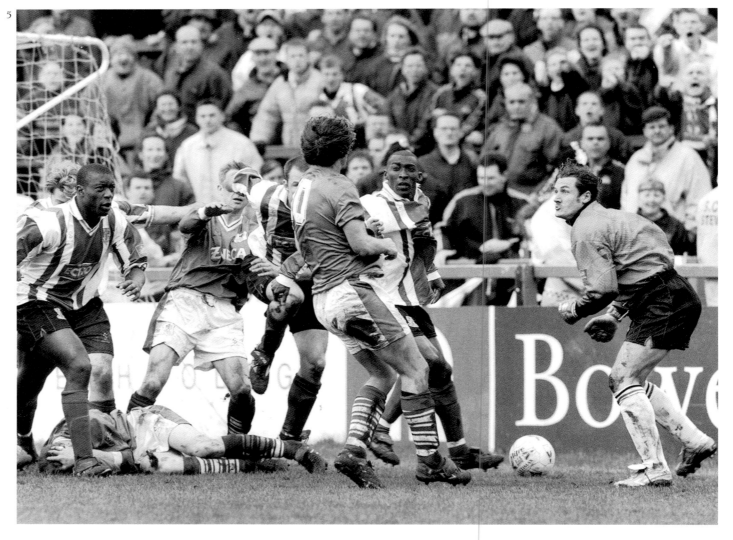

5

6

7

8

An innocuous challenge by Martin McDonald on the Lincoln goalkeeper didn't appear to warrant a free-kick. However the 'keeper, Barry Richardson, kicked out while Martin was lying on the ground and was soon joined by his equally aggressive team-mates. By the time our nearest player, Ben Sedgemore, had got to the scuffle the damage had been done.

More or less every player on the pitch became embroiled in the resulting brawl and even the occupants of both dugouts were involved. When the ref regained control the red card was shown twice. Richardson and Sedgemore were the recipients with a couple of other Lincoln players fortunate to escape punishment.

Sammy and Shane Westley are escorted back to the dugout by Reg Hollis

Pure joy as Lincoln are beaten, this time by a late Steve Wood goal.

As the whole world around them goes into ecstacy, the fan with the oversized cap tells his mother that it's time to go as the game has finished!

The anticipation of a trip to Glandford Park is too much for some people.

Neil gives us a wave

DOH! Leroy Chambers can't score and can't believe it! Another little stumble on the path to glory. Scunthorpe win 1 - 0.

Fans protest after Roarys' recent brush with the law.

Due to a lack of cash, the Youth development programme is put on hold for another year.

Sammy and Peter take charge of training at Kings School playing fields. The players think better of it and try to sneak away while they're not looking.

The Norwegian branch of the supporters club visit for the Barnet game. Former Take That star Robbie Williams (2nd left) gets in on the act.

"Oh Maccy Maccy, Maccy Maccy Maccy Maccy Macclesfield!"

The turning point of the game at Cardiff. Stuart Whittaker comes on and sets up the equaliser after only two minutes

Phil Power celebrates the 2 - 1 win at Cardiff and acknowledges the Macc fans long after the home supporters have gone!

Gil Prescott emphasises the one point that's needed from the remaining two games to ensure promotion.

1.30 and its a sell out for the last home game of the season v Chester.

Despite not being able to play against Chester, Ben Sedgemore does his bit by wearing his comedy shoes to keep the other lads minds from the game.

No turning back......

Ticketless fans are desperate for their own view of history.

Celebrations the Sammy way.

Ryan Price leads the singing during the Chester game. Luckily he won't be giving up the day job.

Job done!

The media return to the Moss Rose - but where's the Mayor?

5.30 While the players celebrate promotion,and interviews are conducted all around the ground, the next generation re-live the afternoons 3 -2 win over Chester

The shadowy figure of Stuart Whittaker warms up at Exeters' St James' Park.

An air of end of term for this one, as pride is all that's at stake.....

.....except for Peter Davenport. His landmark 100th league goal is notched up with little time to spare.

The final kick of the 97/98 season.

The sense of camaraderie that's the Third Division. Supporters greet each other as friends rather than foes.

Exeter fans offer their congratulations and mingle with the players on the pitch. Shirts, socks shin pads are given away....
but Efe's' bandana stays firmly in place.

With only the fourth away win of the season secured Efe Stuart and Steve prepare for the long journey back to Macclesfield.

Only half an hour into the journey and Steve Wood begins to have his clothes re - arranged.

Celebrations from players and fans alike.

"See I told you he'd be here". Gil settles his bet with Sammy as the Mayor puts in his customary appearance

We must go on meeting like this!

"We were only after some comps but he tried to sell us an endowment policy!" For once John Askey fails to score.

They got the Britannia Stadium. We got the trolley AND the chance to play them next season!!

Epilogue

AT the end of May, just over a month since Macclesfield sealed promotion to Division Two, I and Neil met with David to finalise the production of this book and reflect on a fantastic year.

Neil's thoughts inevitably turned to his pride at captaining his club to yet another stunning achievement.

David reflected on the amazing progress the club had made during his three privileged years as Sports Editor on the Macclesfield Express and I enthused about the behind-the-scenes access granted to me in my quest to chronicle Macc's first season in the Football League.

We decided that the naming of this book had been a fairly simple exercise. 'Against All Odds' is a true reflection of the manner of the club's achievement.

They have been the real winners in a sport which is fast being lost to the people who have supported it through thick and thin. The word 'club' is now sadly not particularly apt in describing many teams in the Football League. But it is an appendage which describes Macclesfield Town perfectly.

Spirit and determination has seen the club through to the Second Division from the brink of relegation to the Northern Premier League. Macclesfield Town now stand proudly alongside giants Manchester City and Stoke.

But this roller-coaster journey is showing no signs of running out of steam. New problems will have to be overcome. At the time of writing, the club were desperately trying to hang onto Sammy McIlroy, backers were still reluctant to invest and funds for transfers were slow to materialise.

However, optimism was high in the camp as the players prepared to regroup for yet another trying campaign. Season ticket sales were going through the roof and the Moss Rose was being given a facelift as this unique club readied itself to win promotion to Division One.

Pundits were saying the club had reached as far as it could possible go. But then again they were saying the same 12 months ago. Macc Town proved them wrong last season and against all odds are preparing to prove them wrong and shock the football world yet again.

Paul Atherton